Introduction/1

During the pre-school stage, it is necessary for children to develop skills that will allow them to learn to write in the future. Some of these skills are pre-writing skills which allow children to learn how to hold a pencil correctly and have control of their hand motion when they start to practice writing.

This book consists of a series of exercises that focus on honing fundamental skills children need to develop before they are able to write. The exercises vary from tracing letters, numbers, geometric shapes, general shapes and exercises focused on learning how to draw, copy, identify and color different shapes.

Today, with the existence of new technologies and their frequent use, we stop practicing handwriting using paper and pencil. Writing is an activity of fine psychomotricity, and it is essential to master this skill to communicate through the written medium. Even though we have new technologies that offer great benefits, writing with pen and paper continues to be of the utmost importance in the development of children.

Here are some benefits of practicing writing:

1. When performing the pre-writing exercises, the hand motion is maintained, thus enhancing the brain-hand coordination, giving way to the development of fine motor skills.
2. Concentration is encouraged.
3. It increases creativity, critical thinking, and self-esteem.
4. It helps encourage reading.
5. Facilitates psychomotor coordination.
6. Develops the ability to draw and color.
7. Improves the child's posture.

Ready to start receiving all of these benefits?

Illustrations by Kassandra Sustaita

Traza la línea siguiendo la flecha. Repite el ejercicio varias veces.

Trace the line following the arrow. Repeat the exercise several times.

Traza las líneas siguiendo las flechas.

Trace the lines following the arrows.

2

Traza las líneas siguiendo las flechas.

Trace the lines following the arrows.

Traza las líneas para unir los puntos.

Trace the lines to connect the dots.

4

Sigue el camino sin salirte de las líneas. Repite el ejercicio varias veces.

Follow the maze staying inside the lines. Repeat the exercise several times.

Traza las líneas para unir los puntos.

Trace the lines to connect the dots.

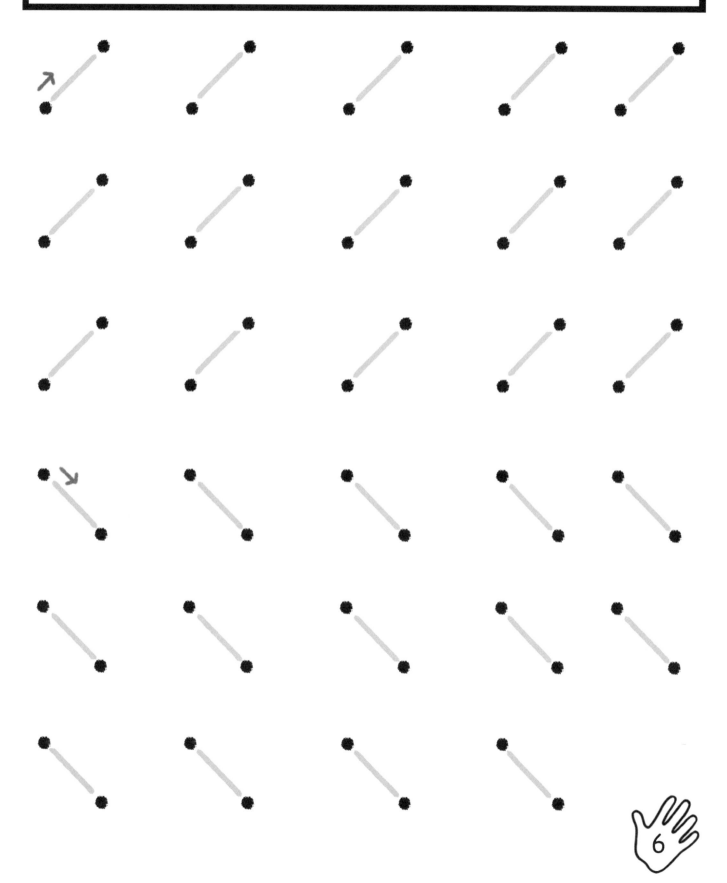

6

Traza la línea siguiendo la flecha. Repite el ejercicio varias veces.

Trace the line following the arrow. Repeat the exercise several times.

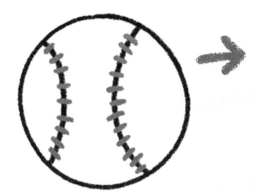

Traza las líneas siguiendo las flechas.

Trace the lines following the arrows.

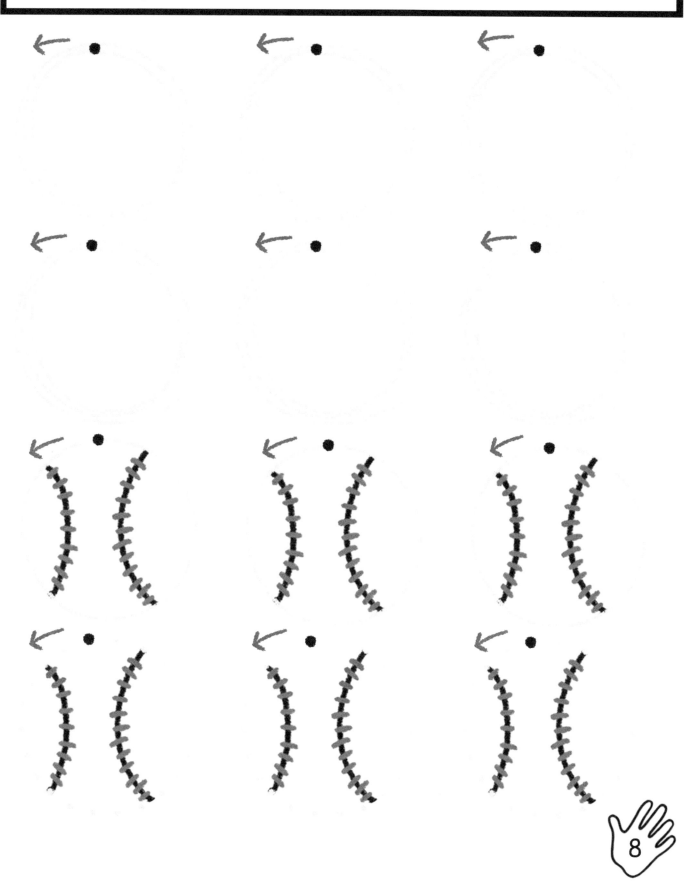

8

Traza las líneas para unir los puntos.

Trace the lines to connect the dots.

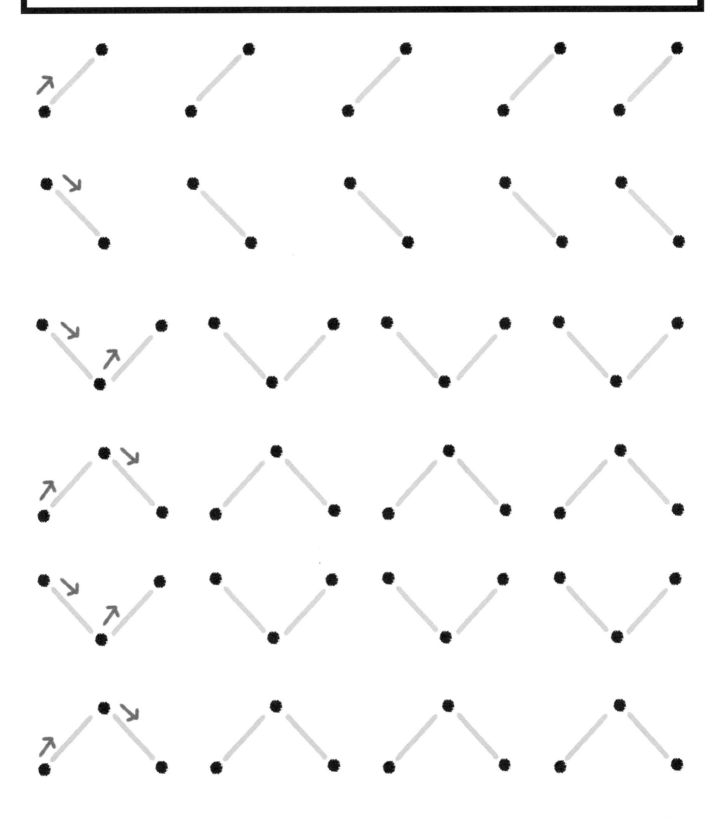

Traza las líneas siguiendo las flechas.

Trace the lines following the arrows.

10

Traza las líneas siguiendo las flechas. Colorea las bicicletas.

Trace the lines following the arrows. Color the bicycles.

11

Traza las líneas para unir los puntos.

Trace the lines to connect the dots.

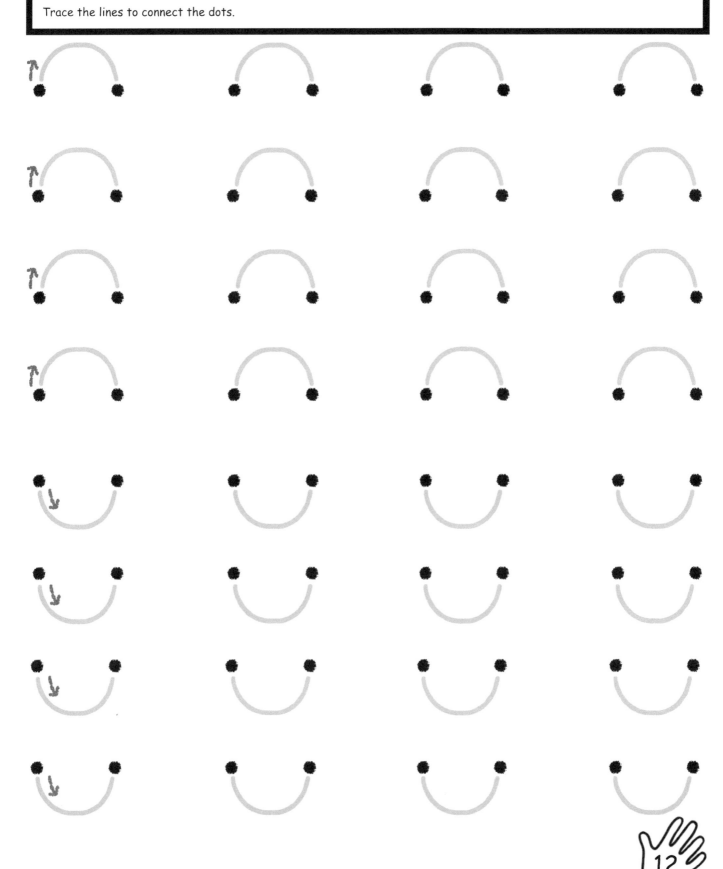

Siguendo las flechas, traza los pétalos de las flores y los rayos del sol. Colorea al terminar.

Following the arrows, trace the petals of the flowers and the rays of the sun. Color the page when your done.

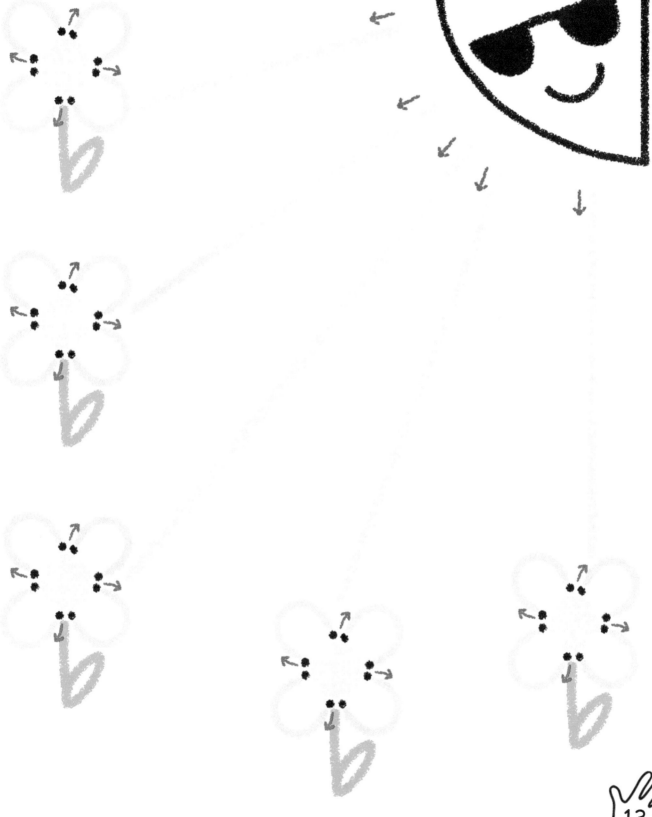

13

Traza las líneas siguiendo las flechas.

Trace the lines following the arrows.

14

Une con una línea los dibujos que son iguales y coloréalos después.

Connect with a line the drawings that are the same and color them after your done.

Colorea la imagen que es diferente en cada conjunto.

Color the image that is different in each group.

16

Traza las líneas para unir los puntos.

Trace the lines to connect the dots.

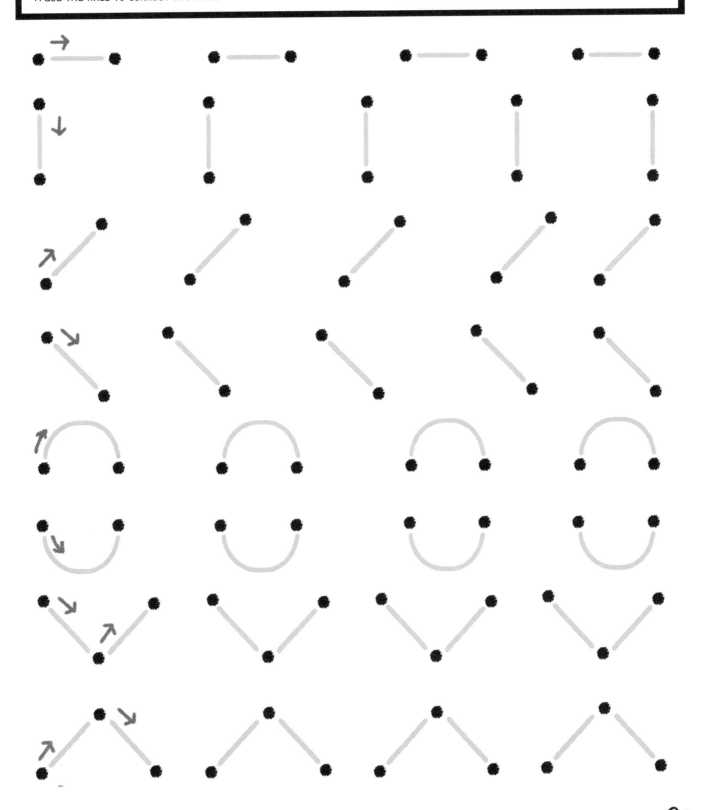

Traza las líneas para unir los puntos.

Trace the lines to connect the dots.

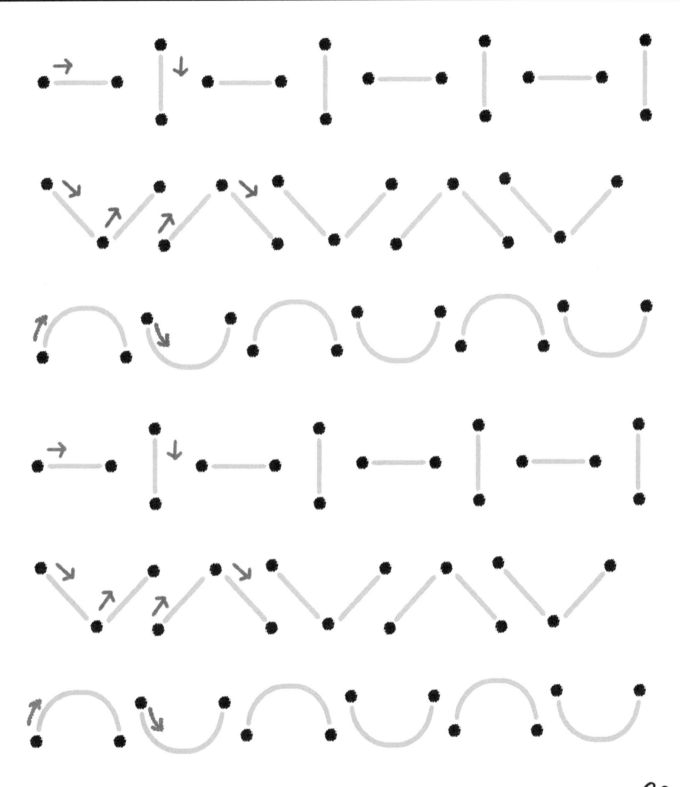

18

Continúa el patrón ABAB coloreando los círculos de cada renglón.

Continue the color pattern ABAB coloring the circles in each line.

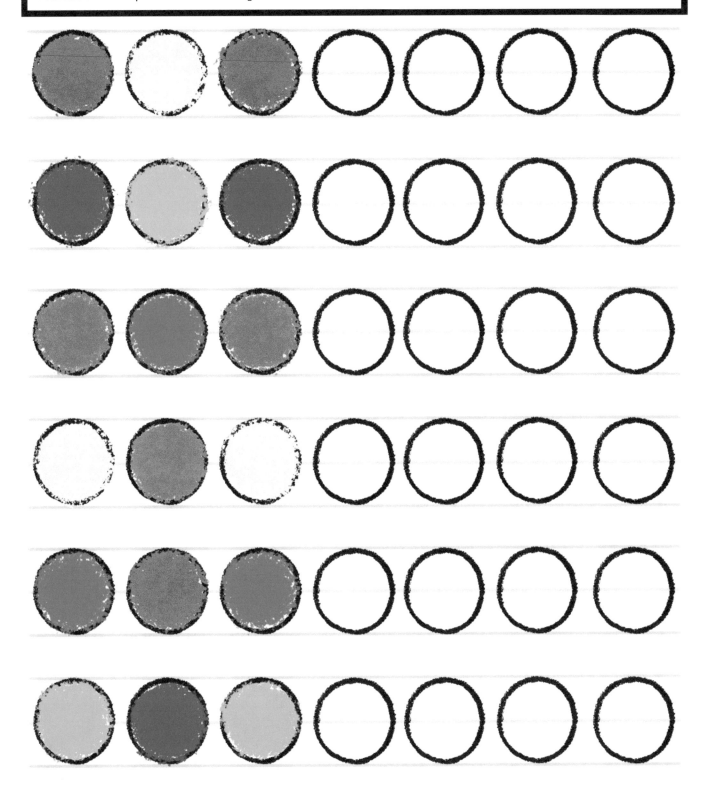

19

Cuenta el número de figuras que hay en el dibujo y escríbelo en el espacio correspondiente. Colorea el dibujo.

Count the number of shapes in the drawing and write the number on the corresponding space. Color the drawing.

Traza las líneas siguiendo las flechas.

Trace the lines following the arrows.

21

Traza las líneas siguiendo las flechas.

Trace the lines following the arrows.

22

Colorea los dibujos de abajo igual que el de arriba.

Color the drawings on the bottom like the one on the top of the page.

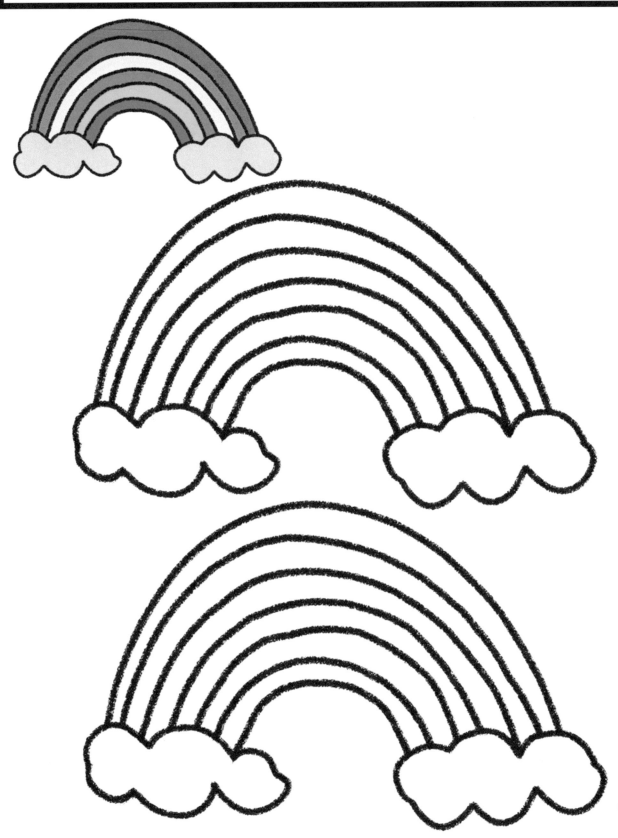

23

Traza las líneas siguiendo las flechas. Colorea el gato y el estambre.

Trace the lines following the arrows. Color the cat and yarn.

24

Traza las figuras y termina el patrón ABAB en cada renglón.

Trace the shapes and finish the pattern ABAB in each line.

25

Colorea las figuras como esta indicado.

Color the shapes with the colors shown below.

Traza las líneas.

Trace the lines.

Traza las líneas.

Trace the lines.

28

Continúa el patrón AABB, coloreando los círculos en cada sequencia.

Continue the color pattern AABB coloring the circles in each pattern sequence.

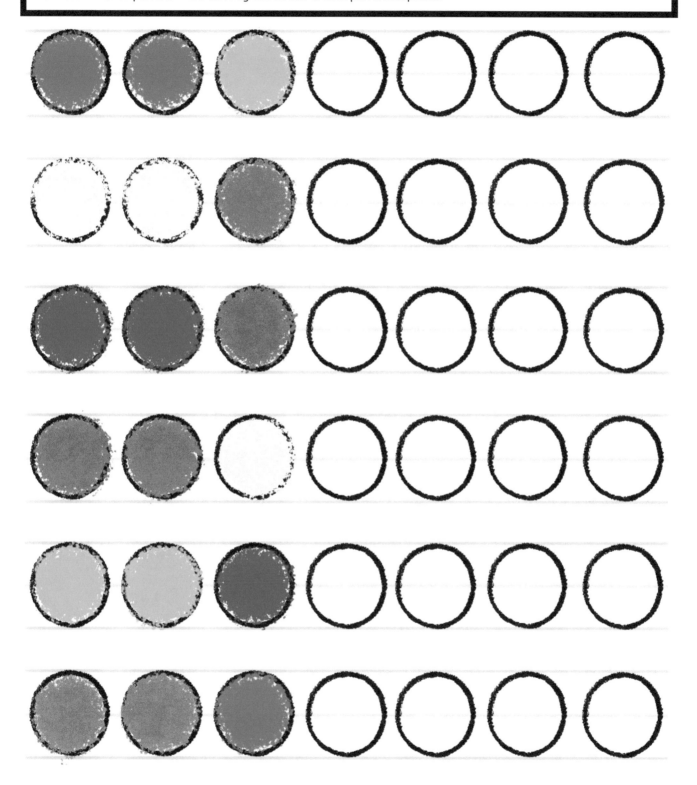

Cuenta el número de figuras que hay en el dibujo y escríbelo en el espacio correspondiente. Colorea el dibujo.

Count the number of shapes in the drawing and write the number on the corresponding space. Color the drawing.

Traza el espiral.

Trace the spiral.

31

Encuentra y traza el camino hacia las zanahorias. Repite el ejercicio varias veces.

Find the right way through the maze to get to the carrots. Repeat the exersice several times.

33

Encuentra la salida del laberinto sin salirse de las líneas. Repite el ejercicio varias veces.

Find the exit through the maze staying inside the lines. Repeat the exercise several times.

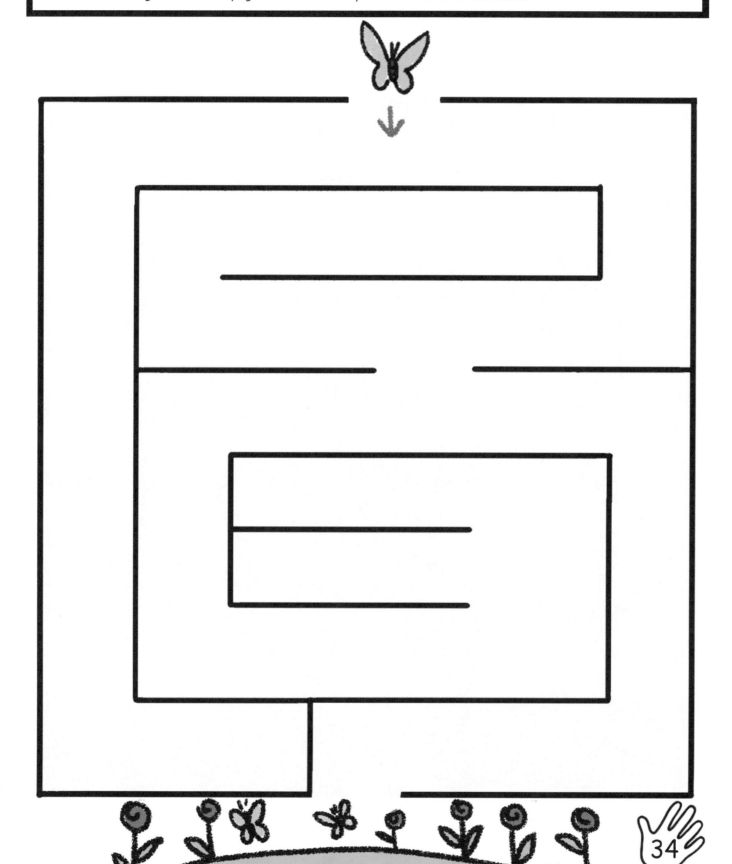

34

Traza las líneas siguiendo las flechas.

Trace the lines following the arrows.

35

Traza el cabello de los niños y termina el lado opuesto. Colorea los dibujos al final.

Trace the childrens hair and finish drawing the opposite side. Color the drawings at the end.

36

Traza las líneas siguiendo las flechas.

Trace the lines following the arrows.

38

Traza los diferentes caminos para llegar a las zanahorias.

Trace the different lines to get to the carrots.

Colorea las figuras como esta indicado.

Color the shapes with the colors shown below.

Traza las líneas.

Trace the lines.

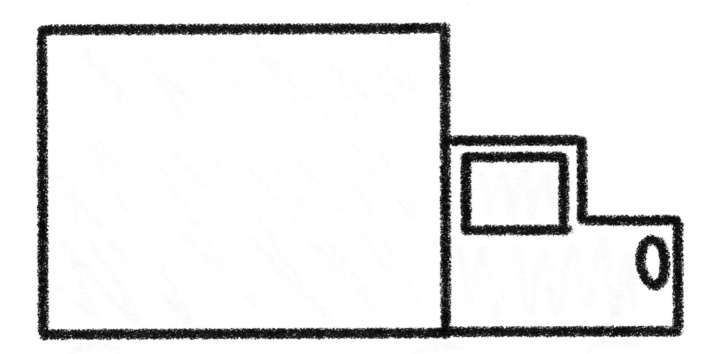

Made in the USA
Columbia, SC
13 August 2024

4044583783700048